BIRD BOXING BIRDS

BIRDS WITH A MEAN STREAK

By

MARTIN LIPAZA

Copyright © 2018

Introduction

Many birds used their wings as weapons, with some evolving special adaptations to be able to engage in combat. They have a wide array of diversifications such as developing bony knobs, spikes or spurs.

There being a debate in some circles for a number of years, in which it is rumored that some birds have enough combat-power to break a person's arm.

Many have adapted over millions of years and are as see them today. From flightless, jousting bird to posturing to fight off opponents, here are just some of the angriest birds, who seem to be in love with the art of boxing.

TABLE OF CONTENTS

Chapter 1. The Mute Swan

The Cygnus olor or The Mute Swan, is the native bird to Eurasia, and was introduced as a species to North America. They are notoriously territorial, sometimes finding just one pair on a small body of water, such as a lake.

They protect their mates, offspring and their nests very aggressively. They start their attacks with a loud hiss, and if this doesn't scare the predator off, they will engage in a physical attack.

They have large bills, which they use to attack predators, and will use their large bony-spurs on their wings to box their opponents.

Chapter 2. Xenicibis

A few millions of years ago, an ancient flightless bird,

the only member of its genus to evolve, could batter

its enemies with its wings, swinging to club its

opponents, like no other bird. Meet Xenicibis.

An extinct, flightless, Jamaican ibis, there were no

marked differences between the males or the females

of its kind. This could mean that both sexes engaged

in this territorial practice.

It is hard to be sure by looking at bones if Xenicibis

used its wings in this way. However, there is

compelling evidence from the bird's arm bones that it

had gone through a process of being broken and then

healing.

From massive calluses forming over fractured wings,

it can be said that Xenicibis used its hands to attack in

defense.

CHAPTER 3. THE PINE SISKIN

The Pine Siskin is a widespread and visible species

across Canada and Northern United States. It forms

large flocks during seasons when it is not breeding.

They have forked tails and short conical bills.

The Pine Siskin are opportunist in nature, and fiercely

defend their territory from any encroachment.

Agile and quick-flyers, when agitated, they react with

aggression and threat-display, raising its feathers and

opening its bill, snapping and grabbing at any and all

intruders.

Chapter 4. The Northern Mockingbird

The *Mimus polyglottos*, or the Northern Mockingbird,

is a native to North America. They are known for their

intelligence and their ability to recognize individual

humans, especially those who have been previously perceived as threats or intruders to their territory.

The males are the first to arrive in a breeding ground to scout and establish territory. They remember and recognise their breeding grounds, and they return to those areas in which they have had the best luck in nesting. And they use a series of courtship displays to attract a female or to pursue a mate.

Once mated, the male and female Northern Mockingbird will defend their nests and surrounding area from other birds or intruders, aggressively.

If a predator is encroaching and is aggressive, the Northern Mockingbirds will call upon other mockingbirds by a distinct call to join in the defense, and the birds will gather to watch the mockingbird

deal with the intruders.

In addition to targeting cats and dogs in general, the

mockingbirds will also target humans at times. They

are unafraid and will target any aggressor, no matter

the size.

Chapter 5. The Great Horned Owl

The Great Horned Owl is sometimes called a The

Tiger Owl, are native to the Americas. When relaxed,

the Great Horned Owl has a fluffy and loose plumage.

But when alarmed, it will pull in its feathers tightly to its body, and their air-tufts will stand up erect on top of their heads. They can flick their tails side to side and when alerts, they will bob their bodies up and down.

When protecting their offspring, or defending itself, the Horned Owl will assume a defensive posture. It will ruffle its feathers, so to appear larger in size to its aggressors, and will lower its head and will spread its wings out, point down and out.

When nesting, the Horned Owl will become so aggressive that they have been even known to attack humans.

Chapter 6. The Rufous Hummingbird

The Rufous Hummingbird or Selasphourus rufus, is a

small hummingbird, with great migratory and

exceptional fight skills. And even though small in its

stature, the hummingbird has a temper, and an equally entertaining shows of aggression.

This behavior can be a problem for other hummingbirds in the surrounding areas, as one aggressive bird can chase away others from a feeing ground.

Their angers flare when they perceive that their feeding or breeding grounds are being violated by unwelcome intruders. Even though all hummingbirds display varying degrees of temper, the Rufous Hummingbird has the most notorious temper of them all.

Their aggressive behavior is at its peak in spring,

when they are defending their nests and claiming

territories.

But the angriest might still go far well into fall, as they

defend their feeding grounds as they prepare to

migrate. A male Rufous Hummingbird will show its

aggression towards feeders, whereas a female will be

aggressive towards anyone who approaches her nest.

They show aggression by loud, fast paced sounds,

and will assume a threat-posture, and try to double in

size by raising its feathers on its head. The

hummingbird will hover over the intruder and then

dive towards them with a loud chirp. They will fight

with their needle-like beaks and sharp talons.

CHAPTER 7. THE AMERICAN COOT

The American Coot is an adaptable water-bird, and

usually they will flock together aggressively and nosily

on open grounds, near ponds.

They possess strong legs, and big webbed feet. They

will rear up and attack other coots all year long, and

towards any other fowl especially during nesting season. And will fight over territorial boundaries with extreme readiness.

The Coot will display four types of aggressive behavior towards all aggressor. They will charge, use a paired-display, spluttering and churning, while competing for resources. And while nesting, the American Coot will defend the territory with the same extreme aggression.

Chapter 8. The Ruby-Crowned Kinglet

The Ruby-Crowned Kinglet is a tiny, olive-coloured

bird which are in a constant restless motion. Lacking

in the species females, the male possesses a hidden

patch of ruby-red feathers on top of its head, which it raises when it gets excited.

It is quite easy to elicit aggressive behavior from the Kinglet. When he sees the red feathers being displayed by other males, or a predator, the instinctive reflexes trigger their own flashing of feathers. Or whenever in the presence of a female.

Chapter 9. The Southern Cassowary

The Cassowary is a native of Papua New Guinea. They are very shy birds, and often are able to disappear before even being detected. But when provoked, they are able to inflict grievous injuries, which have proved to be sometimes fatal to humans and dogs.

Cassowaries have small wings, with stiff, porcupine-like quills, and they sport a dagger-like claw on each second finger. This is particularly worrisome since they sometimes kick humans and animals.

The male cassowary will defend its territory and its mates, whereas the female will defend hers and other overlapping territories with several other male partners.

Chapter 10. Why Birds Get Angry?

Birds will get angry when anyone intrudes on their nests. Whenever one gets near a breeding area, the birds view that as a predatory action and instantly become aggressive.

Birds go to great lengths to keep their offspring, their mates and their feeding grounds, safe. And they will aggressively defend any perceived predator, fiercely.

If food is scarce in the area, the nearby birds will display even more aggressive behavior than usual.

This is evident when Cardinals and Robins see their

own reflection in windows and attack because they

think it is another bird encroaching on their grounds.

Nature is wonderous and awe-inspiring. Learning

about birds and other animals, brings us a feeling of

calm and also provides us a glimpse into our own little

worlds. Which we may find, resembles theirs as yet.